Carving and Painting
An Heirloom Santa

Paul F. & Camille J. Bolinger

Photography by Pat McChesney

Schiffer Publishing Ltd

77 Lower Valley Road, Atglen, PA 19310

Acknowledgements

A special thanks to Pat McChesney for the excellent work photographing while we carved and painted. Thanks also to the crew at Super Color in south Spokane for handling our photo developing.

Printed in China

ISBN: 0-7643-0194-2

Book Layout by Michael William Potts

Published by Schiffer Publishing Ltd.
77 Lower Valley Road
Atglen, PA 19310
Phone: (610) 593-1777 Fax: (610) 593-2002

Please write for a free catalog.
This book may be purchased from the publisher.
Please include $2.95 for shipping.
Try your bookstore first.

We are interested in hearing from authors
with book ideas on related subjects.

Preface

I am delighted that my friend, Paul Bolinger, has decided to join Schiffer's stable of carvers.

I would like to say that I had some influence on Paul, but he had been a successful carver long before my first book came out. He was represented by several prestigious outlets at that time and was considering leaving his responsible position with a semiconductor firm in California.

I had the honor of doing a show with Paul in California soon after he had made the scary move to full-time carver. I was amazed at the people who were taking numbers to get a chance to buy his beautifully carved creations.

I know you will want to try Paul's unique method of carving and Camille's method of painting, so please join me in thanking them for sharing their talents.

Ron Ransom
Santa Carver

Contents

Left side view of Gustave.

Introduction

What makes something a potential heirloom? This is a tough question and the answer largely depends on an individual collector's taste. Over a period of time, however, some common qualities that confer heirloom status can be defined by observing collectors.

The common factors that seem to help define something as having heirloom potential are quality, uniqueness, style, definite present value, and something I call warmth. If an item can meet the following criteria, it may be said to have "warmth" — the item reminds the collector of "the old days," the artist is known and the collector knows something about the artist, and, the most elusive, the object seems to have value that will carry on into the future.

Our Santas definitely have heirloom potential. They are made of quality materials that will last and they have a style that should transcend fad and fickleness. Original carvings sell for substantial amounts so they have recognized present day value. They have a tie to the past that evokes visions of Christmas past. They are definitely unique.

Their unique and recognizable style is a big part of their wide popularity. A collector can walk into a shop anywhere in the country and pick our work out immediately because of the style.

In this book you will learn how to carve and paint an heirloom Santa in the style we have developed. I will demonstrate the use of the tools I normally use to carve and my wife will demonstrate the techniques she has perfected for oil painting. This does not mean that you must use the same tools I do nor are you expected to paint exactly the same way she does. Remember, it's not the method but the result that makes a work unique. Your style is your signature.

I hope you find great pleasure in creating your own heirloom Santa — something you can keep in your family and pass down the generations. After you have completed the Santa shown in this book I encourage you to try others on your own. The aspect of the process that leads to a unique style is commonly referred to as "design" and we are as much designers as we are woodcarvers and painters.

You should work to find your own voice. Developing your own designs and your own style will not only make your work unique, but will also be extremely satisfying to you. Please remember that all my work, original and reproduction alike, is copyrighted. This book is provided for you as an aid to learning. The designs shown in this book should not be copied or used for any commercial purpose.

The figure that will be carved is named Gustave the Stout. He is related to Gustave the Gusty, who is one of the figures that is in reproduction. You might find it helpful to purchase a figurine of Gustave the Gusty, or one of our other figurines, to use as a study aid in this or future projects. These are available in stores around the country or directly from me. (See the gallery section of this book.)

Gustave the Stout is a European looking Santa dressed in a long coat reaching all the way to the ground. He sports a hood on his head instead of the more American stocking hat. There are many styles of Santa that I carve ranging from these very European likenesses to more American images with red coat, pants, and black boots.

Look carefully at the pictures of Gustave before you begin to carve so that you will have a firm mental image of the final figure. Of course you will have the book and pictures as reference, but a firm mental picture is your best assurance of success. I'm sure you have heard the remarks attributed to the old master sculptors, about carving away everything that isn't the subject so that the subject just magically appears. Well, there is some truth to that concept, but only if you have a firm mental image of the subject.

Look at Gustave's hood and see how it sits on his shoulders and the shape of it as it rises up to a point toward his back. Note the designs and decorations.

Study his face for a moment, looking closely at his mustache, nose, lower lip, and eyes.

Look at Gustaves's overall shape. He is more or less a cone rising from a wide base to the tip of his hood. This is one of the easiest shapes to carve since it allows you to work with the grain of the wood.

Look at Gustave's coat. See how it opens in the front to reveal pants inside. Note the tips of his boots poking out at the edges of his coat. Look at the fir trim around the base of the coat.

Notice the very upright posture of Gustave. This standing figure, with its straight up and down orientation, is the most straightforward. The figure is balanced around the natural centerline.

Gustave was carved with minimal decoration. This was done to prevent distracting you from the figure and it's simple lines. You may certainly add whatever decoration you wish on your figure.

Front view of Gustave.

A Gustave Pattern. Actual size is 14' x 5 1/4'. Enlarge this drawing 200% to achieve actual size.

Typical tool set for Santa carving.

Tools

I have run into many carvers over the years and their attitudes toward tools seem to range across a wide spectrum. On the one hand, there are those who are definite tool freaks; these guys are much more concerned with the tools than with what they can produce. I sometimes wonder if they ever actually get anything done. On the other hand, there are those that take great pride in using nothing but a knife. I find myself in the middle. To me tools are to be used, not collected.

I purchase tools because of the shape needed. There are many adequate brands available and I have not yet ended up preferring one brand over the other. I generally shop mail order for my tools since, at the moment, there are no local suppliers where I live. I find that the tools offered by mail order catalogs do the job for me.

Since I made the move to professional carver, I have eliminated some tools. I now have a minimum set of tools that I can use to carve any of the creations I design. You must remember that when I travel I take my tools with me so portability and simplicity are critical considerations for me. Excluding a table, everything else I need to set up and do a carving demonstration packs into a single soft sided sport-type bag.

I have included a tool list that shows all the tools I use. The asterisk indicates the minimum tools recommended for this project. Of course I know that I'll get a letter down the road from someone who says he did the whole thing with nothing but his granddaddy's rusty scout knife and some really gnarly fingernails. Just remember that the tools aren't the point — the project is the point.

Tool List

Tool #	Size	Type	Special Shape	Required
#3	20 MM	Gouge	Fishtail	
#4	16 MM	Gouge	Fishtail	*
#4	12 MM	Gouge	Fishtail	
#4	10 MM	Gouge	Fishtail	*
#4	6 MM	Gouge		
#1	6 MM	Chisel	None	
#10	3 MM	U Gouge	None	
#7	3 MM	Gouge	None	
#41	6 MM	V Parting	None	*
Micro	1 MM	V Parting	None	
Micro	3 MM	V Parting	None	*
		Knife		*
		Dividers		*
		Torpedo Level		*
		9/16 Drill Bit		*
		7/16 Drill Bit		*
		1/4" Drill		*
		Cordless Drill		*
		Pencil		*

Sharpening system with 4 wheels.

Sharpening

Certainly the most common problem for woodcarvers is sharpening. I can't count the number of woodcarvers who have asked me for sharpening tips. Working with dull tools is not only uninspiring but also dangerous. I believe that dull tools are the reason for the many people who try woodcarving but soon give it up.

As a professional woodcarver, I use my tools all day long. Time is definitely money, so I can't afford lengthy sharpening techniques. I usually sharpen my tools every 10 - 15 minutes when working in my shop. Sharp tools are critical to quick, controlled carving.

Years ago I was introduced to a sharpening system at the Frankenmuth Woodcarving studio under the instruction of Georg Keilhofer. Since then I have purchased two versions of the system from Georg and the first one has been in use for over 10 years.

The system I use includes a series of motorized wheels on a single spindle. My primary sharpener has four separate wheels mounted on a single motorized spindle. There are two general types of wheel on the system: one "grinding" stone and three polishing wheels.

The "grinding" wheel on this system is a synthetic material with abrasives embedded in the artificial matrix. The wheel's working surface is flat. This wheel removes metal quickly and is used for final shaping on the tool. It also allows a little "undercutting" at the edge of the tool which I find makes it sharper.

The remaining wheels are rubber wheels, both flat and shaped, that have a polishing compound vulcanized into them. As the rubber is eroded by the tool being sharpened, polishing compound constantly comes to the surface of the wheel. The shaped wheels allow me to polish the inside of "V" and "U" gouges, as well the outside, in a matter of seconds. The flat wheel allows me to polish the shallower fishtail gouges I use.

When I go on the road I can't take the motorized wheels with me so I have to revert to the old fashioned strop with aluminum oxide to keep my tools ready. Believe me, I am glad to get back to my shop and my sharpener when the trip is over.

Other systems are available and apparently they work. I am very happy with the methods I learned and would recommend them to anyone.

These systems can tend to be expensive for the hobbyist. It is possible for a carving group or club to get together and purchase a single system that can be kept at or brought to the meeting location so that carvers can periodically refresh their tools.

Mallets

Years ago I used wooden mallets and thought they were "cool." The tap, tap, tap of the mallet seemed as much a part of woodcarving as everything else. Once I began to spend more hours at the bench, however, the noise became a problem.

Now I use the urethane coated mallets offered by the various catalogs. This type of mallet reduces noise and impact so your hands and arms are strained less. I prefer a 12 ounce mallet, but that is just my preference. The lighter mallet sometimes requires me to hit a little harder when roughing out a project but I use a mallet many hours each day, so weight is important to me.

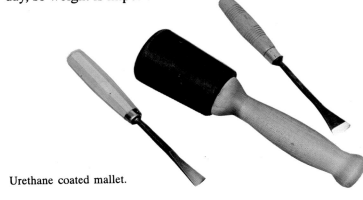

Urethane coated mallet.

Carver's arm. 4" X 4" oak.

Securing the Work

Holding the work piece securely is one critical aspect of carving. Since I tend to use gouges instead of knives, I prefer to have the work secured on a fixture so that both hands are free.

There are many types of fixtures available today for securing your work. The one I prefer is the combination of the woodcarver's arm and the woodcarver's screw.

The arm itself is nothing more complicated than a 4" X 4" piece with a slot drilled and cut into one end. The commercially available carving arm I use has a complicated "elbow" joint that I never use. I would recommend a straight arm instead. You can easily make a carving arm for yourself.

The woodcarver's screw is a combination wood screw and machine screw. The wood screw portion is turned up into the bottom of the work piece until it is secure. The handle is then threaded onto the machine screw section and turned up against the carving arm until it is tight. I always put an oversize washer between the handle and the wooden carving arm since the unprotected wood can easily be chewed up by the constant loosening and tightening of the screw handle.

I clamp the carving arm directly to my workbench. This is a more secure method that holding the arm in the workbench's vise. You can generate some pretty hefty whacks with the mallet when you get going, so you definitely want the work to be secured.

One side benefit of this method is a reduction in the damage to one's hands and fingers. What woodcarver hasn't cut himself or herself? Well, with both hands freed from holding the work you rarely find a hand in the wrong place.

Leveling the Work

Since most of my work is done "by eye," it is imperative that the work piece always be perpendicular to the horizon — the level workbench. The Santas are primarily 14" to 24" tall. The taller the piece, the more critical is the leveling. There are lots of variations possible when clamping a work piece onto a carving arm which has been clamped onto a workbench, so I always level the top of the carving arm before securing the work piece in place.

In the early days, I would take my workbench to outdoor art and wine festival settings to demonstrate woodcarving. The first few finished pieces carved in the great "unlevel" outdoors were definite "leaners" when I got around to displaying them on a level table in my level house. I soon learned that a level is one of the critical tools in my bag.

Carver's screw with handle and oversized washer.

Inserting the carver's screw into the bottom of the work piece. The carver's screw shown here is a 3/8" model. I drill a 1/4" pilot hole for this screw. The handle doubles as a wrench for driving in the screw.

Screw with handle and washer shown assembled and in the bottom of the work piece.

Level on top of the carver's arm.

The Work Piece Centerline

The serious Santas I carve are generally upright and balanced around a centerline. This tends to make the piece more formal which is the look I prefer.

Providing a centerline also allows for ease of balancing right and left features in a bilateral carving and keeps the figure perpendicular.

The centerline must be kept throughout the process. I generally carve an area and then redraw the centerline before I move on to a new area. I will often use the level in the vertical position to assure that my centerline remains truly perpendicular to level as the work progresses. A set of dividers is also critical to keeping the piece balanced.

Centerline marked on piece.

Lighting

It would seem that having adequate lighting would be common sense but I will mention it anyway. Shadows can fool your eyes. A project can quickly become a problem when you can't visually judge what is level or the relative depth of cuts because of the shadows. In my shop I have installed 14 double tube 4' long fluorescent lights in the ceiling. The pattern is such that there are lights everywhere around my bench; there are no shadows. Maybe you guys with younger eyes don't have to worry about this, but the rest of us should take the time to get adequate lighting even if it is just a portable light.

Finding the centerline.

Workbench

There are two workbenches in my main carving area. The one I use predominantly is set up so that I can work standing up or at least sitting on a tall stool. I prefer standing since it helps me keep my back and neck from developing strain during the long hours of carving.

The workbench is secured to the top of a box I constructed of 2" X 10" material. The box contains 150 pounds worth of sandbags to help hold the bench in one place. Whatever type of workbench you have, make sure that it is secured or weighted, otherwise you will be chasing it around the shop.

If you have a wooden floor, your best bet would be to secure the bench to the floor which should make it about as stable as it can get.

Front view of the workbench, showing the carving arm clamped to the bench with pipe clamps.

Wood Selection and Preparation

I use kiln dried Basswood for all the carvings I do since we have found it carves well and is very accepting of the painting techniques used by Camille. I recommend that you use Basswood for this project since you will be learning the painting techniques perfected for Basswood.

The wood piece used for this project has an initial size of 4" X 6" X 14" and is a single piece. You may glue up pieces but that will affect the painting that comes later and all glue lines will show on the finished product.

Be careful to select the wood with the straightest possible grain. Take the time to look since this will affect the final quality of your carving.

For carvings that I am attempting for the first time, I cut the wood to size, taking care to make sure that the bottom of the work piece is squared with the sides of the piece. This will give the best possible chance for establishing and maintaining the centerline as the piece is carved.

Rough Outs

When doing production carving, I primarily use rough outs that have had the majority of the waste material machined away. Enough material remains that each piece can be customized but the roughing out saves me time. All rough outs are done from my originals to my specifications and are not from commercially available rough outs.

Occasionally in the past I have used precarved blanks, of my own designs, which have been machined to the approximate final size. These precarved blanks are approximately 50% finished. I have established a supply of these precarved blanks for Gustave the Stout which may be purchased directly from me. (See the gallery section of this book.)

Sawing the Piece

I do not own a band saw, so I make all my initial cuts with a hand saw. When a project is smaller, I often make no saw cuts at all but just plunge in. For this project, I will show how to make the cuts with a hand saw.

If you have a band saw, you may certainly speed up the process of sawing out the blank piece. Just adapt the instructions provided here to "round" your cuts and save time.

The finished dimensions are 4" X 5 1/4" by 13 7/8" excluding the hands and walking stick which are added to the piece.

Carving the Santa

The process of carving the Santa involves multiple passes and is similar in concept to peeling an onion. I take little bits from all over the Santa and then return to the starting point and do it again. Taking larger cuts or working down to final size in a single area can easily lead to mistakes. Peeling the onion will allow you to keep all parts of the figure in balance and proportion.

Use your largest gouge to carve down from top to the stop cut. The waste should come out in big chunks.

Mark the shoulder lines on the sides, 10" up from the bottom. Mark vertical lines 1 3/4" out from centerline in each direction.

Continue removing until all waste wood is gone.

Saw into the block on shoulder line to make a stop cut.

Cut and remove waste from over the other shoulder.

11

Mark the underside of the left arm 6 3/8" up from the bottom at the elbow (back) and 5 3/4" up from the bottom at the wrist (front).

Mark the underside of the right arm up 6 3/8" from the bottom at the elbow (back) and up 6 1/4" up from the bottom at the wrist (front).

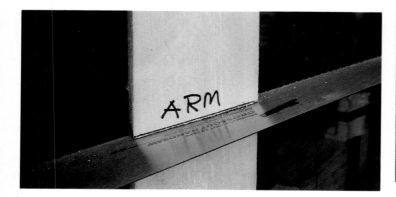

Saw along the bottom of the left arm for a stop cut. Depth 1 1/4".

Use your largest gouge to carve up to the stop cut and remove waste.

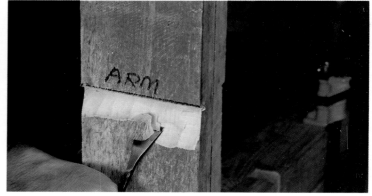

Saw along bottom of right arm to make a stop cut. Depth is 1 1/4". Remove the waste wood to the full depth of the stop cut under the arm.

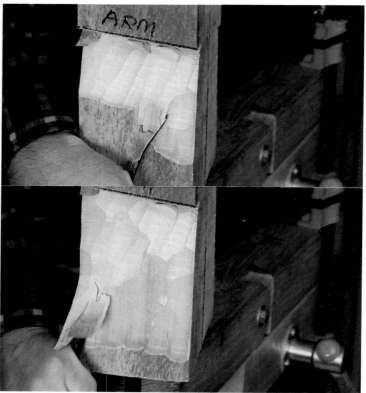

Taper the body up from the very bottom to under the arm. At the bottom the body will remain the full original size.

Remove the waste from under the other arm. You now have defined your block. You should see the head, shoulders, arms, and body in block form.

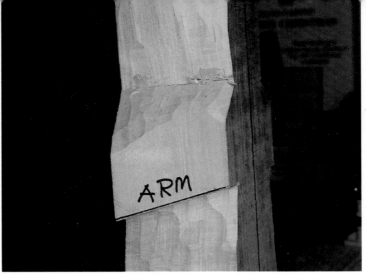

Round the tops of both shoulders.

Use your dividers to mark a vertical line 1 3/4" from the back to define the upper arm (biceps).

Use your largest gouge to begin rounding the shoulders and tops of the arms. Don't take too much, this is the only the first pass. You will gradually reduce the size of the block over time.

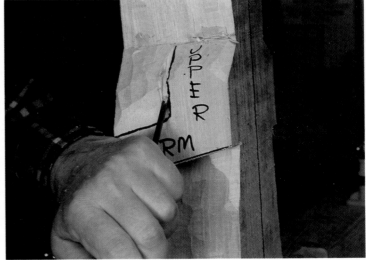

Use a "V" gouge to cut the vertical line from inside the elbow to the top of the shoulder. Cut 1/4" or so deep.

13

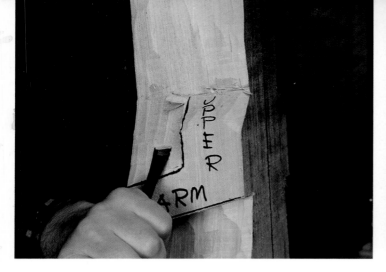

Use a large gouge to remove the wood in front of the biceps. Angle cuts upward with the grain. Keep recutting your vertical groove with the "V" tool to define the biceps.

This is the front view with the waste removed from both arms. Don't worry, we will slim the arms down later. Remember that we are peeling an onion.

Mark the biceps line on the other arm.

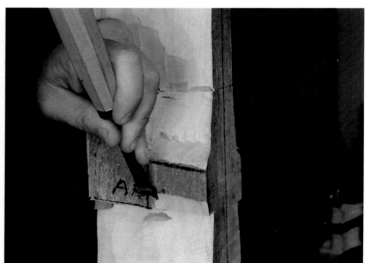

Using a large gouge to cut downward, begin rounding the bottoms of the sleeves.

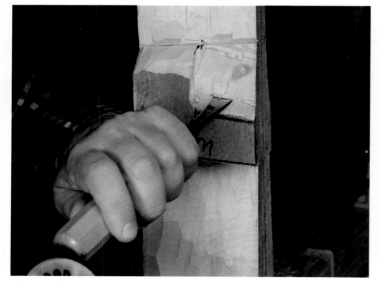

Remove the excess from this arm. Don't try to do it all at once. You'll be back later.

View showing the rounded bottom of the right side sleeve.

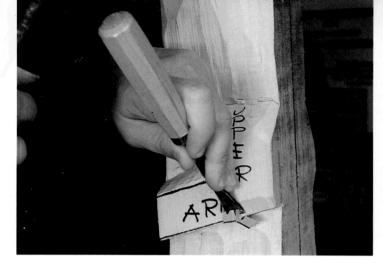

Round the bottom of the other sleeve.

Using a large gouge, begin tapering the hood from the front to the top of the rear and from the shoulders up to the centerline.

Draw in the rough area where the face will be carved. The bottom of the beard is 6 1/4" up from bottom of the piece. The sides of the face are 1 1/2" out from the centerline each way. The top of the face is 2 3/4" down from the top of the piece.

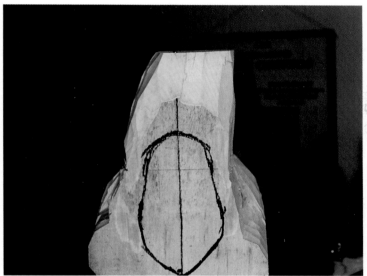

One side tapered.

Connect the centerline from front to back along the top to give yourself a visual reference.

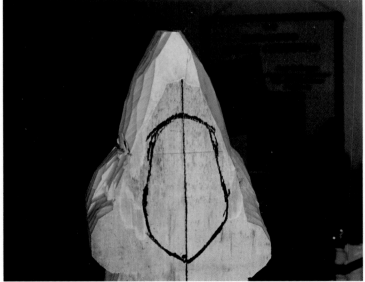

Both sides tapered.

15

Hood tapered from front to rear. Note that the back has not been touched.

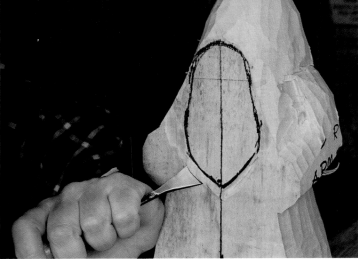

Use a large gouge to cut upward and begin removing waste from under the beard. Don't overdo it. You will be back to trim it down again later.

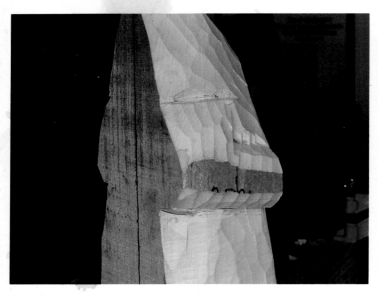

This view of the back shows that it has not been touched.

Use your dividers to mark the insides of the sleeves 1 1/2" in from the outside of the block.

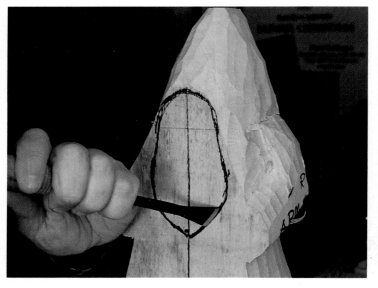

Use your largest gouge to make stop cuts around the lower part of the beard.

Use a medium gouge to outline the inner edges of the sleeves by making stop cuts.

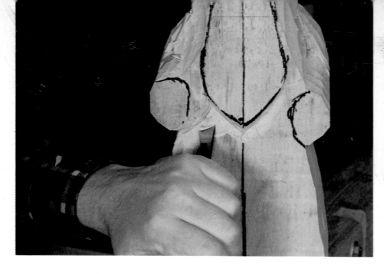

Begin removing waste wood from under the fronts of the sleeves and the beard.

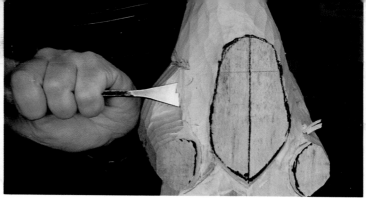

Remove waste from in front of the biceps too.

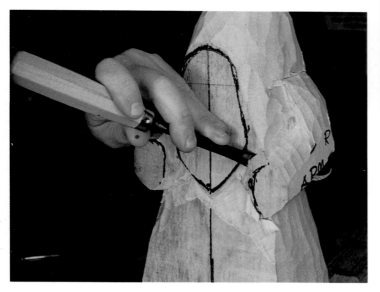

Work both arm areas to keep the piece in balance.

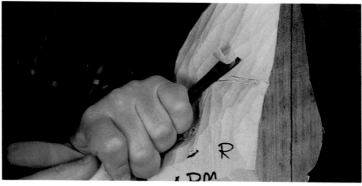

Work the hood, shoulders, and arms all over lightly to reduce them closer to their final size. Peel the onion.

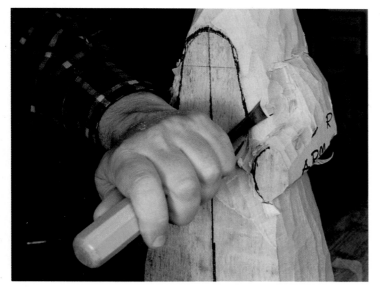

Return to the upper arm and remove some more waste. Don't get too ambitious, you will be back once more.

A view of the back at this stage.

Use a "V" gouge to cut a shallow groove separating the inside of each sleeve from the beard.

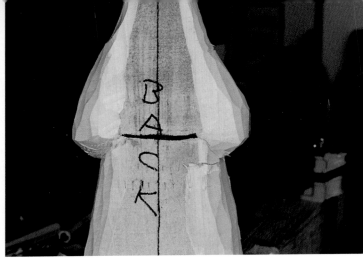

Mark a line across the back 7" up from the bottom and inside the elbows.

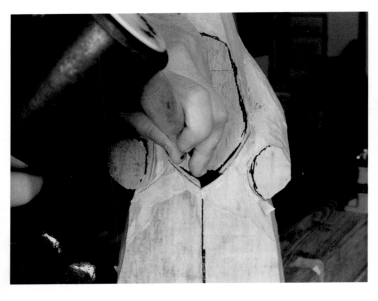

Deepen the stop cut around the bottom of the beard.

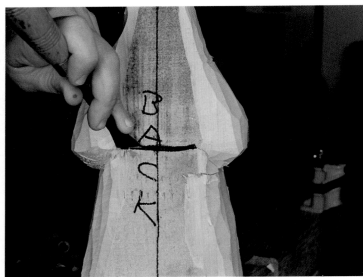

Make a stop cut on the line about 1/2" deep.

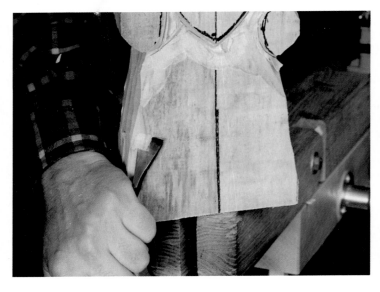

Begin to shape the lower body upward to the stop cut. Leave the bottom of the piece roughly the original size.

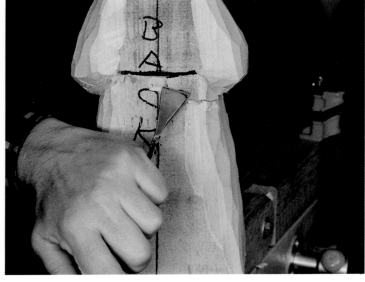

Cut up to the stop and remove waste from the lower rear of the coat.

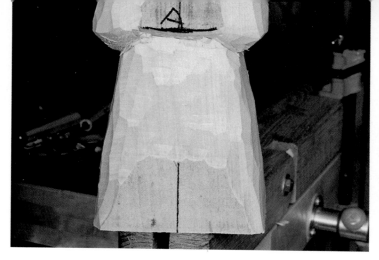

Taper the lower coat up to the stop cut. Don't overdo it. You will trim it more later.

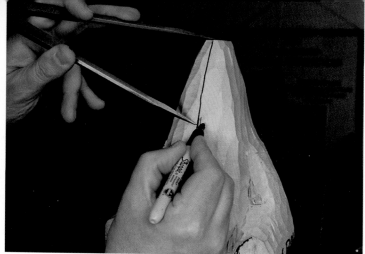

Move to the front and measure down 2 3/4" from the top and mark where the top of the face will be.

Very lightly trim the back of the hood.

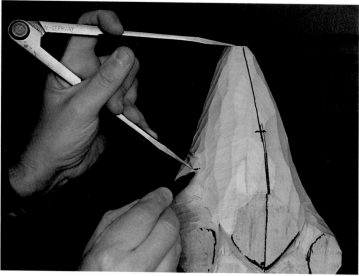

Measure down 4 1/2" from the top to each shoulder.

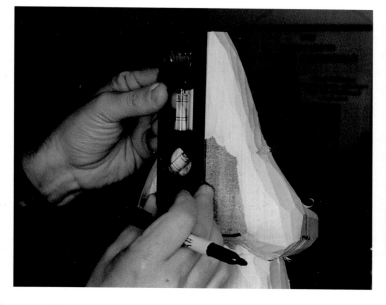

Establish the centerline on the back using your level.

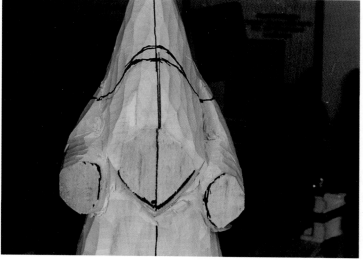

Draw in the outline of the hood bottom. Note: Ignore the double line in the photo; I made a mistake and redrew the line. Use the top line as a guide since it has better placement and shape.

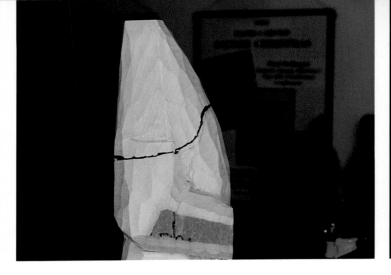

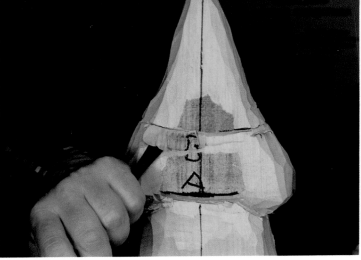

The hood continues around the sides and back of the figure. You can "eyeball" the line.

Cut up to the stop cut all the way around. Don't overdo it.

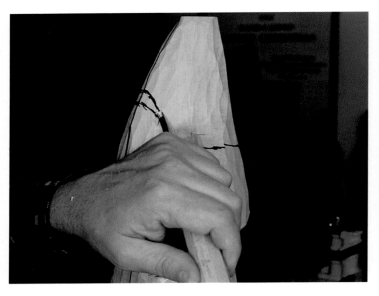

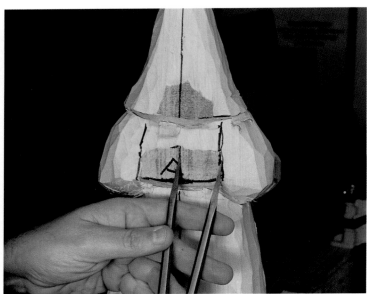

Use a "V" gouge to outline the hood all the way around the figure.

Move to the back and measure out 1 1/4" and mark the inside of each sleeve at the elbow.

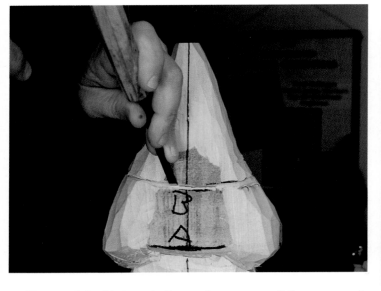

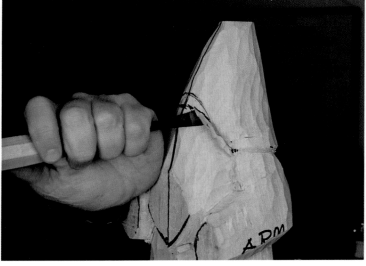

Use a straight chisel or a knife to make a stop cut all the way around the hood bottom.

Continue cutting waste away from the bottom of the hood.

Use a larger gouge to shape the sides of the beard.

Trim the tops of the arms to the crease.

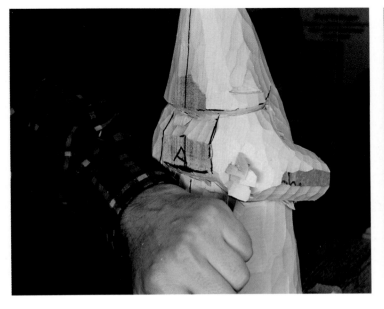

Round the backs of both biceps with a large gouge.

Begin tapering and shaping the beard with a medium gouge.

Use a "V" gouge to cut the crease inside the elbow.

Taper and shape the beard and the face area. Don't overdo it.

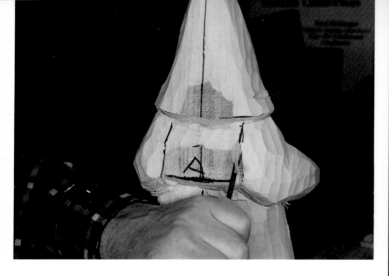

Use a "V" gouge to cut the grooves on the inside back of the sleeves.

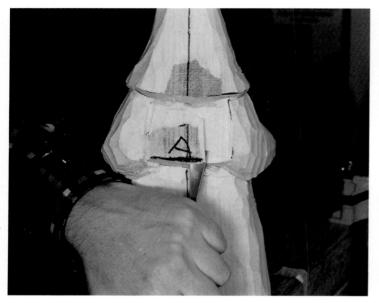

Remove the excess wood from the back between the arm grooves.

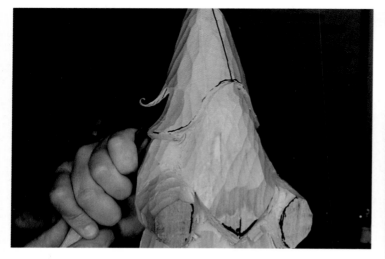

Use the largest gouge to carve into the hood above the shoulder, then up to the tip of the hood. This defines the shape of the hood. Start up 1/4" or so on the hood so that the remaining piece drapes the shoulder.

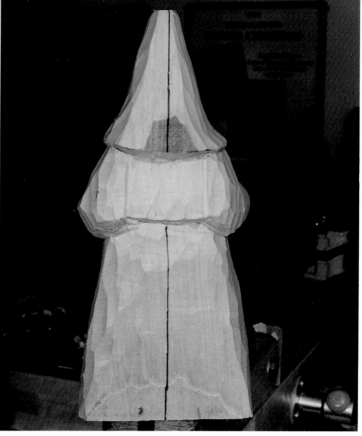

This is the back view at this point.

Return to the sleeves and reduce them to their final size. From top to bottom they should be about 1 1/2".

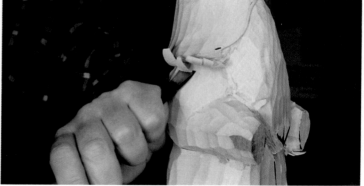

Trim up the tops of the shoulders and biceps.

To begin making a notch at the back of the hood, use a large gouge to cut into the back of the hood about 1/2".

Trim down to the notch.

Cut down to meet your upward cut and form a notch in the back of the hood.

Clean up the notch. If you have a "U" gouge, this would be a place to use it and cut across the notch side-to-side.

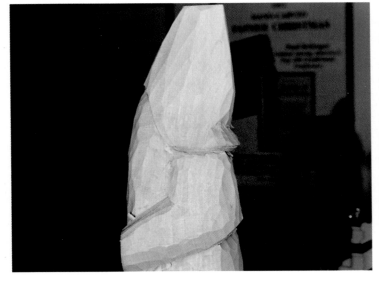

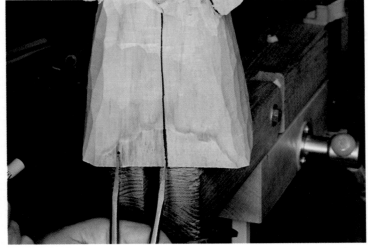

This view shows the notch carved into the back of the hood.

Measure 1 1/2" out from the centerline each way at the bottom. I actually made my marks farther out but your piece will look better this way.

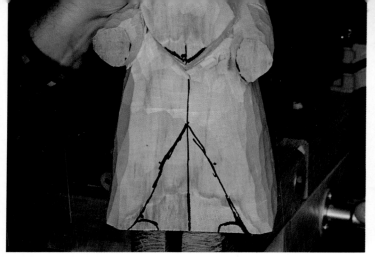

Draw a triangle from your marks up to a point on the centerline 4" up from the bottom. Draw the tips of the boots in at the bottom. Eyeball the right size and position for your boot tips.

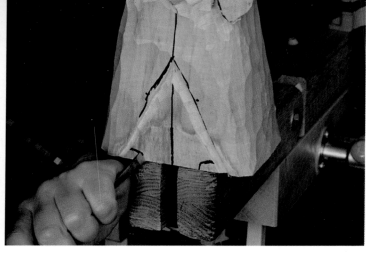

Use a medium gouge to outline a stop cut around the boot tips.

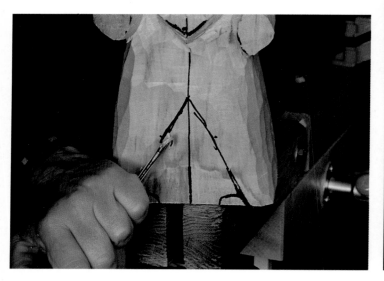

Use a "V" gouge and a chisel or knife to make a stop cut along the lines at the front to open the coat.

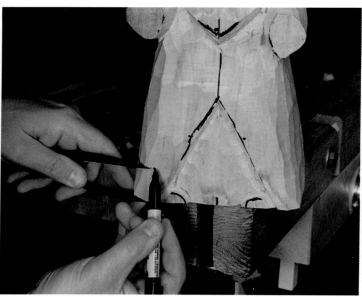

Measure up 1 1/4" from the bottom and mark.

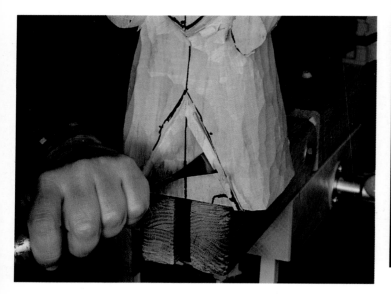

Use the largest gouge to remove the waste up to the stop cut.

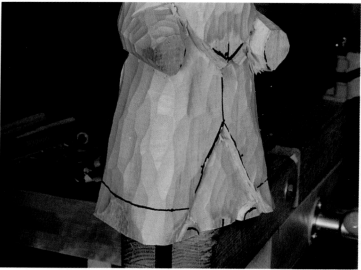

Mark a line completely around the figure at the 1 1/4" height. This will separate the coat from the fur that will be carved at the bottom.

Use a "V" gouge to groove completely around the figure.

Trim the "fur" around the entire figure, cutting by "eyeball."

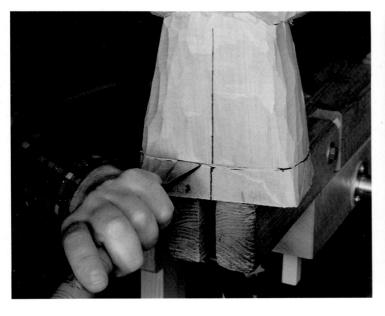

Use a large gouge to set a cut in to the fur line.

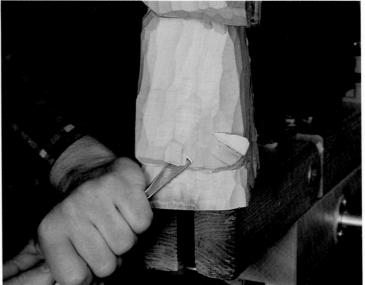

Trim the coat above the fur using a large gouge. Shape the body all the way up to the bottoms of the arms, beard, and cloak. Trim and shape by "eyeball."

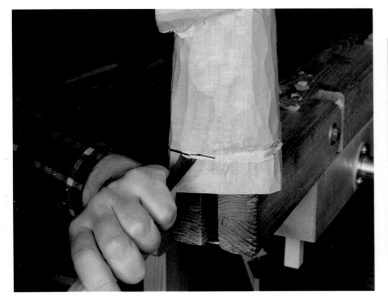

Carve up to the stop cut or groove. Don't go very deep.

Deepen the stop cuts under the arms, beard, and the back of the cloak with a straight chisel or knife.

Trim and taper the lower body once more to these deeper cuts. Shape to your liking. I left my figure very bulky since he is to be named Gustave the Stout.

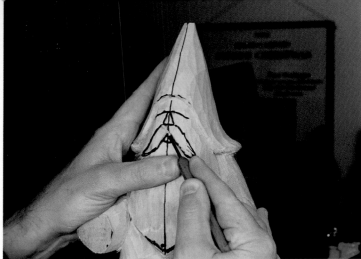

Use a micro "V" to outline the facial features along the lines you have drawn.

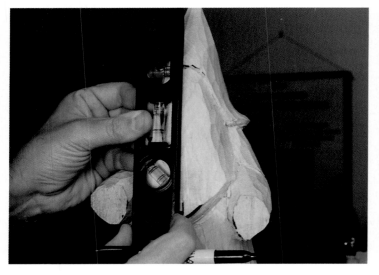

Establish the centerline on the front and back.

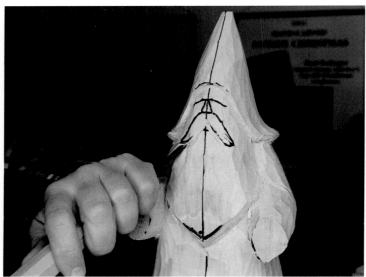

Use a medium or small gouge to carve up to the mustache.

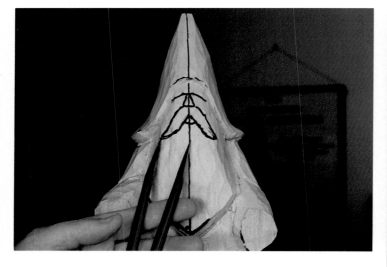

Draw the face onto the figure. Use dividers to make sure it is balanced from side-to-side and forehead to mustache tips. Measurements won't help with this. You should draw it the way you see it. Redraw it if you don't like your first try.

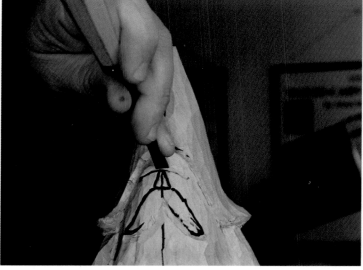

Use a medium gouge to set a stop cut over the eyes and define the brow. Don't overdo it. Work on the face should be slow and careful.

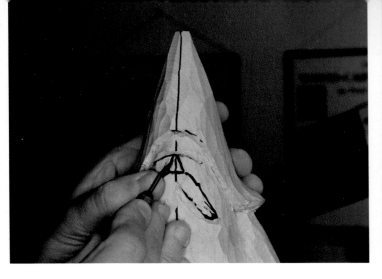

Use a micro "V" to run grooves up along the sides of the nose.

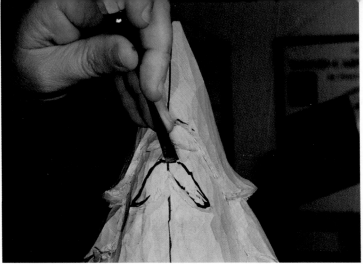

Make a stop cut under the nose with a medium or small gouge.

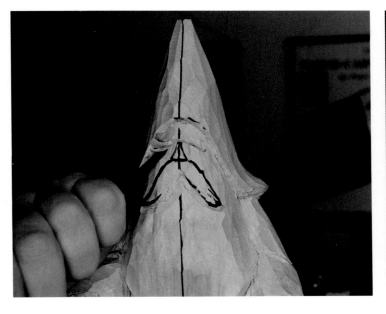

Use a medium or small gouge to remove the excess wood from the eye area.

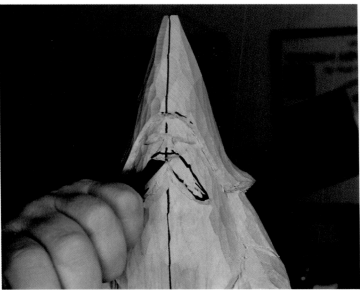

Cut up under the nose, removing the excess mustache.

Use a medium or small gouge to trim up into the "bridge" area of the nose.

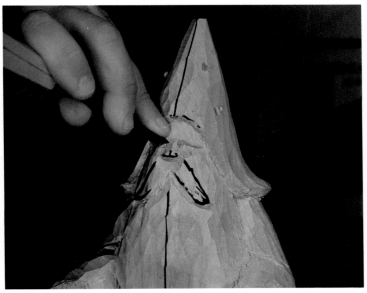

Recut the stop cuts over the eyes.

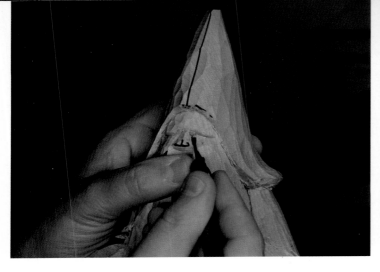

Recut the sides of the nose with a micro "V".

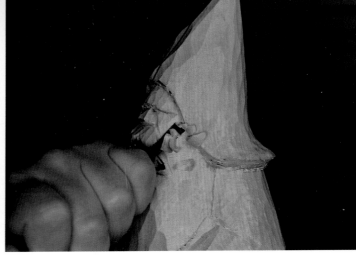

Trim up the cheeks and the sides of the beard.

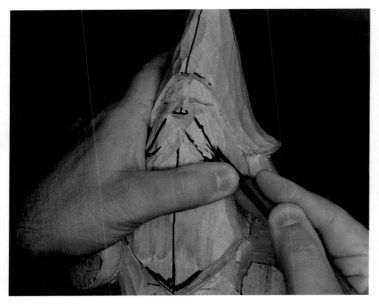

Use a micro "V" to define the top of the mustache.

Deepen the stop cut under the mustache with a knife or chisel.

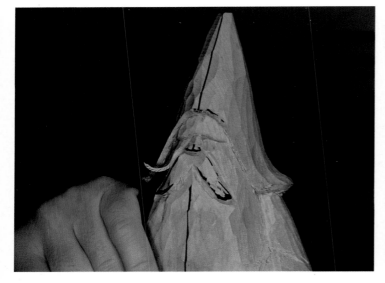

Use a medium or small gouge to cut wood from the cheeks above the mustache.

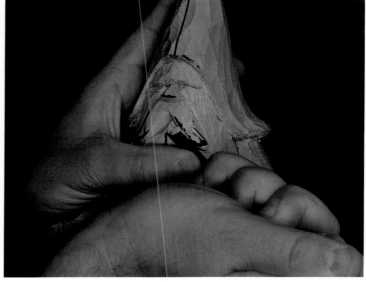

Trim the excess away from under the mustache.

Trim the excess away from the mouth area.

Trim away the excess beard from below the lower lip.

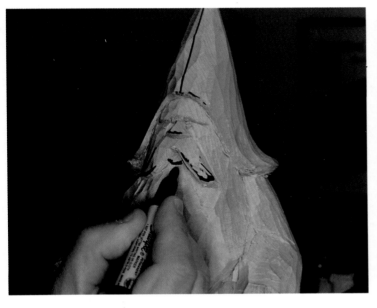

Draw in the line under the lower lip. Any shape you prefer. Note that the upper lip does not show on this carving.

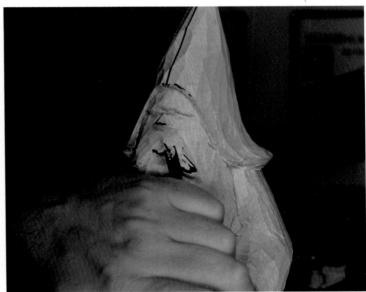

Trim the mustache to the shape that pleases you.

Use a medium or small gouge to set the stop cut under the lip.

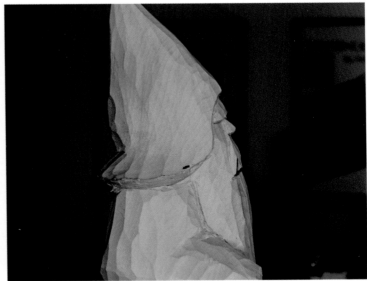

This side view shows the face at this point.

Front view at this point.

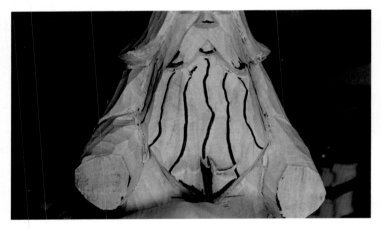

Draws lines on the beard. Carve grooves with a "V" or micro "V".

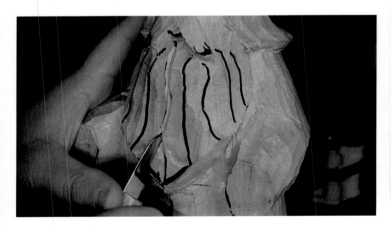

Cut deeply into the grooves with a knife.

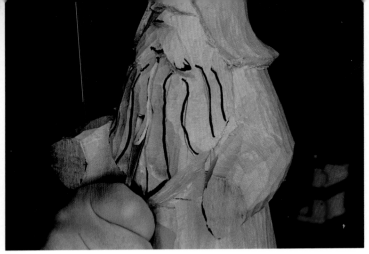

Carve both sides away from the knife cut to deepen the grooves in the beard.

View of grooves partially cut into the beard.

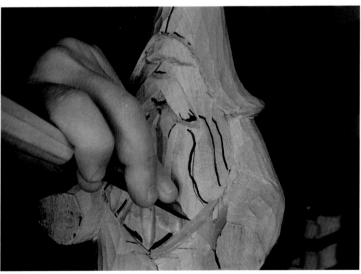

Use a large gouge to curve the tips of the beard and to separate beard "strands" at their tips.

30

Use a large gouge to cut open the strands at the center of the beard. This adds a little interest to the beard.

Using the micro "V," cut above the eyebrows and between the eyebrows to define them.

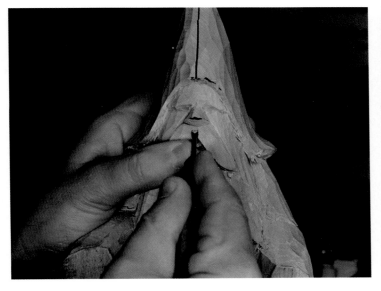

Use a micro "V" to carve the line up the middle of the mustache.

Carve the forehead back under the hood.

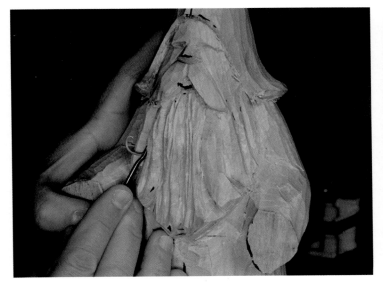

Use a micro "V" to carve the hair lines into the beard. Go as deep as you wish.

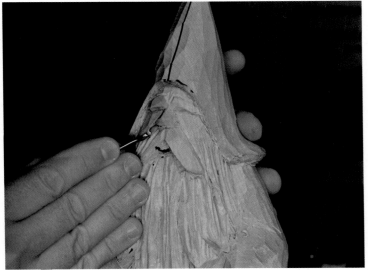

Use the micro "V" to put lines onto the mustache.

This is the front view at this point.

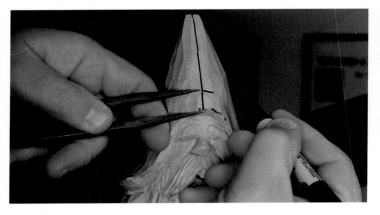

Measure up 5/8" from the forehead in front and on the sides of the hood.

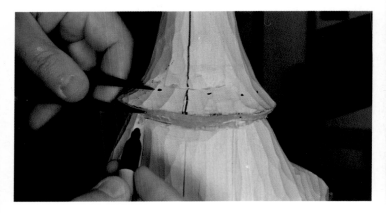

Measure up 5/8" on the back of the hood. Draw a line all the way around the hood at the 5/8" height.

Use a micro "V" to groove along the marked line on the hood.

Use a medium gouge to remove the excess wood above the groove and to shape the hood.

Remove the wood above the groove all around the front and sides of the hood. Shape the hood by "eyeball."

Use dividers to help draw a holly leaf (or other) pattern on the front of the hood. There is no specific measurement here. Do it to your liking.

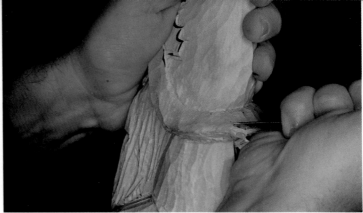

Use a medium or small gouge to cut down and round off the edge of the hood.

Use the micro "V" to outline the holly leaves.

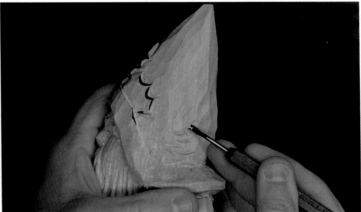

Use a micro "V" to cut squiggly grooves laterally across the hood to simulate a cloth pattern.

Use a medium or small gouge to cut the excess away from the leaves.

This view shows the finished hood with the pattern grooved into it.

Use your dividers to help balance a design on the back of the cloak. I have chosen a heart resting on leaves.

Use the micro "V" to cut the inner lines on the design.

Use a small gouge to outline the design.

Remove the excess wood with a gouge and shape the edges of the heart and the leaves.

Use the small gouge to remove the wood from around the design.

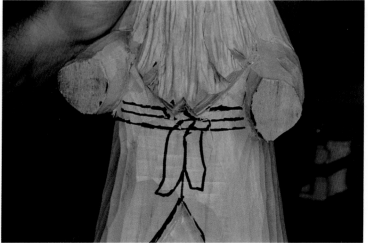

Use your dividers to help draw the belt or rope around the waist. The top of my rope is 6 1/4" up from the bottom. The rope is 1/2" wide top to bottom.

Use a "V" gouge to groove the top and bottom of the belt/rope all the way around the figure. Be careful to leave the rope ends hanging down in front.

Use a straight chisel or a knife to set in a stop cut above and below the belt/rope.

Remove the excess wood above and below the belt.

Use the micro "V" to outline the dangling rope ends.

Use a small gouge to remove the wood from the sides of the rope.

Use a small gouge to put a stop cut at the end of the rope.

This is the back view at this point.

Cut a groove to divide the rope into 2 loops using a micro "V".

Use the micro "V" to cut lines on an angle on the upper and lower rope loops to simulate the twisted strands of rope.

Draw a design hanging from the belt. I chose a heart because hearts are my wife's favorite. You can do anything you wish.

Outline the design with a small gouge.

Remove the wood around the design with a small gouge.

Shape and smooth the design with a small gouge.

Cut away any excess wood on the coat. You are still slimming at this time.

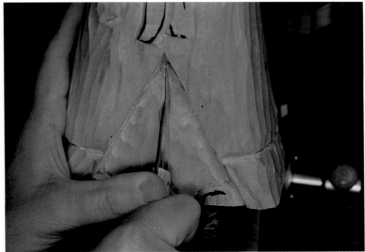

Use a knife to cut a deep groove on the centerline dividing the pant legs.

Use a medium gouge to cut away the sides of the knife cut to separate the pant legs.

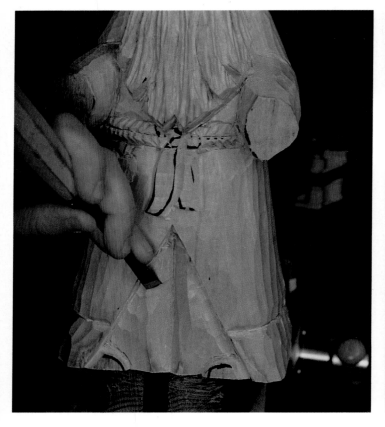

Use a large gouge to put horizontal or almost horizontal cuts into the pant legs where you want to make wrinkles.

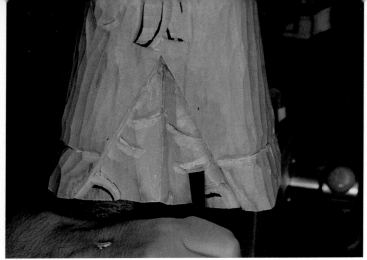

Cut wrinkles into the pant legs. I don't measure these, I just cut them where they will look good.

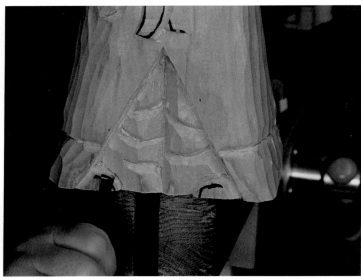

Cut back and round the tops of the toes of the boots with a small gouge angled upwards.

Use a micro "V" to cut the groove separating the sole of the boots from their uppers.

Cut down to nip off the edge of the coat at the very bottom. This undercutting will make a stronger edge and prevent later chipping.

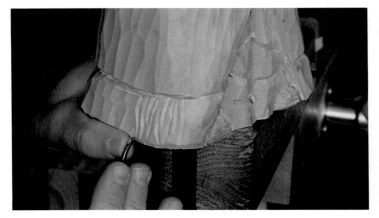

Use a micro "V" to cut vertical grooves simulating a fur trim around the base of the coat.

Mark back 1/4" from the end of the sleeve and cut off the excess.

Drill holes into the sleeves with a 9/16" bit. Go in about 1 1/2".

Use a "U" gouge to create angled cuts into the drill hole to simulate the sloping of the sleeve opening. At this point you should look the whole piece over to see if the shape pleases you. You should do any additional "sizing" or decorating at this point so that the figure is the way you want it. Clean up any burrs or chips with your knife.

39

This is the front view before cleanup or sanding.

This is the back view before cleanup or sanding.

This is the side view before cleanup or sanding.

This is the side view before cleanup or sanding. I use a Foredom setup with various ruby or diamond tips to do the initial sanding of the grooves on the piece. I then hand sand two or three times with various grits of paper ending up with a 400 grit paper. I try to get the piece smooth but without erasing the tool marks. I feel that the smoothness simulates old age and wear. It also helps my wife keep from losing the hairs on her brushes.

You may also clean up the piece with a knife by slowly going over all the cuts and grooves to remove the "chips and burrs."

Draw the right hand on a 1" X 1" basswood stick. On this carving, the right hand will be holding a walking stick. When I work on hands I usually hold the piece clamped in the vise of my workbench. At some points it is necessary to unclamp the piece and hold it in your free hand.

Drill through the hand with a 7/16" bit. Be careful not to split the bottom when the drill bit exits the piece.

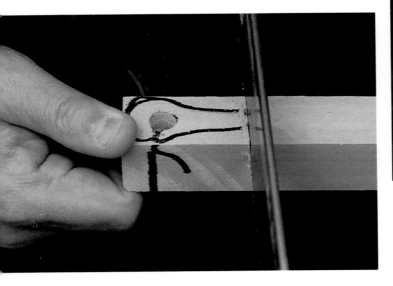

Saw a stop cut at the wrist about 2 1/2" from the end.

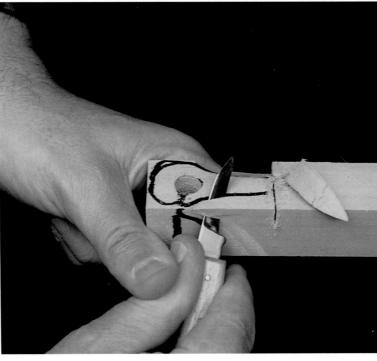

Use a knife to shape the hand back to the stop cut.

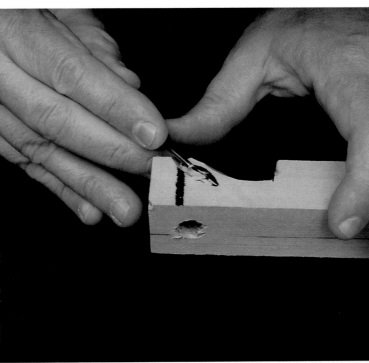

Rotate the hand 1/4 turn. Draw the thumb onto the hand and outline with a micro "V" gouge.

41

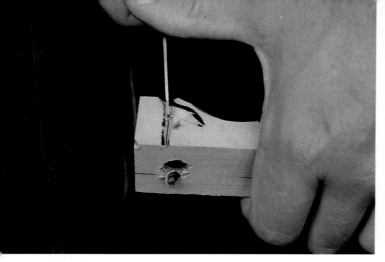

Cut a groove across the hand to define fingertips.

Cut away a little wood at an angle to form the fingertips.

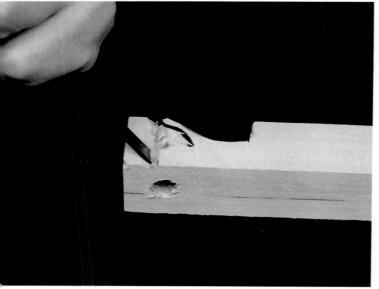

Use a small gouge to carve away the excess wood all the way down to the drill hole.

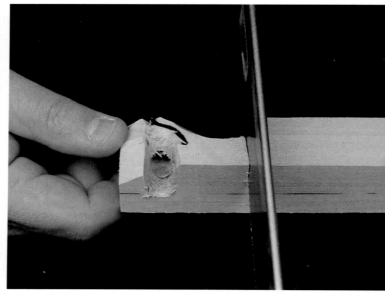

Saw a stop cut at the wrist.

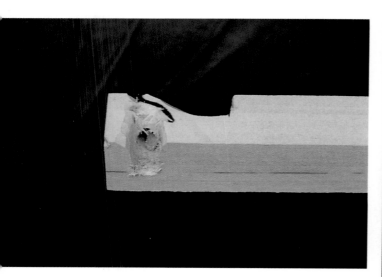

This is a view of the hand with the wood removed down to the drill hole.

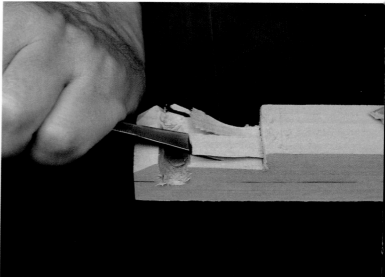

Shape the wrist.

Rotate the arm 1/4 turn to show the bottom. Cut a stop cut at the wrist.

Rotate the hand 1/4 turn so that the back of the hand is up. Make a stop cut.

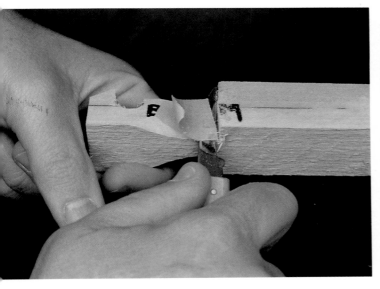

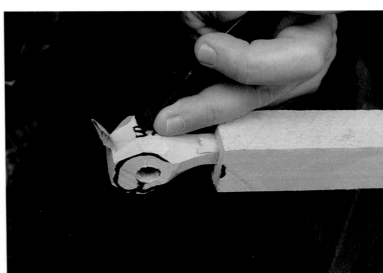

Shape the wrist.

Cut away the wood from the knuckles.

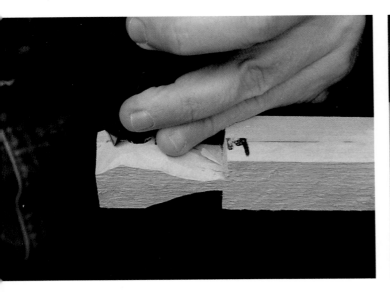

Cut away the wood to shape the bottom (or trailing edge) of the fingers.

Hold the piece in your free hand and shape it into the final shape with a knife.

Draw lines between the fingers. Use a micro "V" to groove the separation between the fingers.

Make a stop cut at the tip of the thumb with a small gouge.

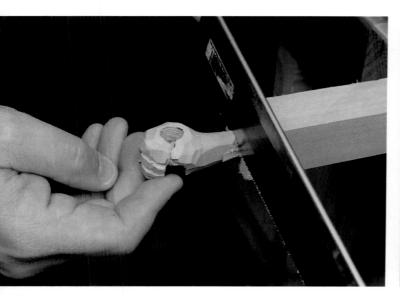

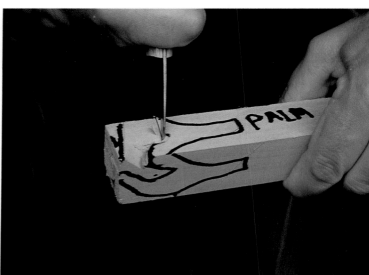

Cut the hand off at the wrist. Clean it up with your knife or Foredom and sand it.

Cut across the palm to form a crease.

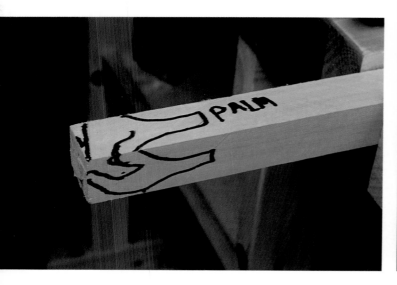

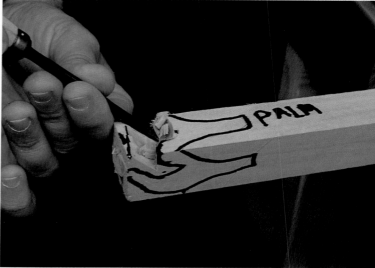

Draw the left hand on the stock with the palm side up. Sure, you can look at your own hand. I do it all the time.

Use a gouge to remove the wood from the palm and to shape the fingers.

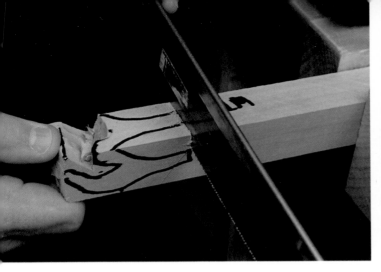

Make a stop cut at the wrist.

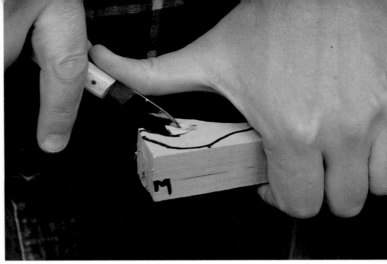

Rotate the hand 1/4 turn and use a knife to cut the wood from under the thumb. Be careful, the wood is not too strong here.

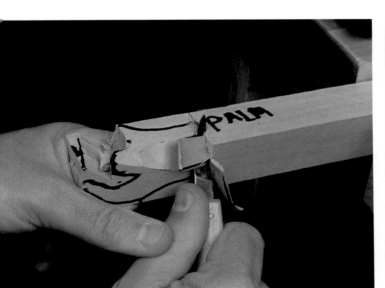

Shape the thumb and wrist.

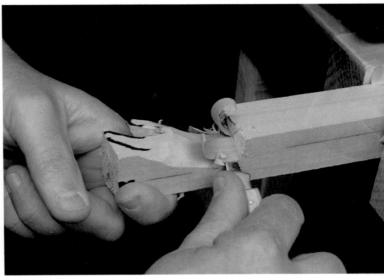

Make a stop cut at the wrist and shape it with a knife.

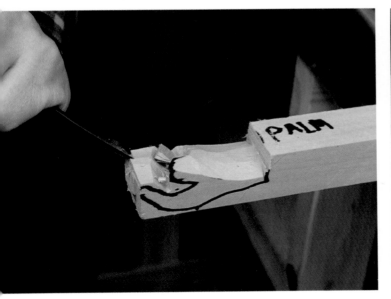

Finish shaping the fingers to the palm.

Hold the piece with your free hand and shape the back of the hand with a knife.

Use a knife to cut fingertips to shape.

Draw the inside of the fingers and cut with a micro "V".

Cut a stop cut and shape the wrist.

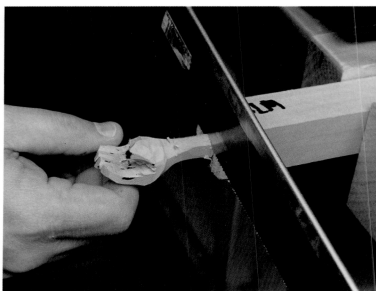

Cut the hand from the stock. Clean it up with a knife and then sand it.

Draw the lines separating the fingers. Cut the grooves with a micro "V".

Cut a thin piece of basswood 8 3/4" long. Carve the top end round so it fits up through the hand. Make cuts into the stick to simulate an old walking stick. Sand the walking stick.

Front view of the finished, sanded carving.

Back view of sanded carving.

Left side view of sanded carving.

Side view of sanded carving.

Painting the Santa

The painting technique shown in this chapter is one that Camille has experimented with for several years. Some years ago she read an article about oil painting on wood in a magazine and began to experiment. She has pretty much perfected this technique and has created some beautiful Santas over the years.

The basic technique is one of wet over wet. A base coat is applied to precondition the wood for the color coats. The color coats are applied over the base coat while it is still wet so that maximum penetration and depth of finish are achieved.

Since this technique uses oil paint there can be no wood filler used on the carving. Wood filler rejects the oil paint and will show as a blemish. You should work with the best wood you can find and be careful in the carving.

Camille prefers Grumbacher Pre-tested Artist oils for this technique. The thinning agent is boiled linseed oil. Brushes are flat natural bristle #10, #6, #3, and a #2/0 detail brush. She uses styrofoam plates for palettes since they are cheap and disposable. Camille uses the same brushes for each color but cleans them between colors with odorless paint thinner.

You should work in a well ventilated area when working with oil paints. The lighting is critical; natural light is best but the most important thing is to have plenty of light.

WARNING: Spontaneous combustion is possible when working with oil paints, linseed oil, paper towels, and cloth. Immediately after you have finished cleaning up your brushes, thoroughly soak the paper towels or cloths you used in soapy water before disposing of them.

The first step is to prepare a base coat for the piece. I pre-mix my base coat and keep it in an 8 oz. plastic cosmetic bottle with a close-able pull-push top. The base coat is mixed from a 2" line of raw sienna squeezed from the oil paint tube into the bottle. I fill the bottle to 2" of the top with boiled linseed oil. Make sure the lid is secure. Shake the mixture well (5 minutes). I use styrofoam plates as palettes and to hold the base coat. A single carving will use about 2 oz. of the mixture.

I wear plastic disposable gloves to protect my hands and to keep fingerprints off the work. Use a #10 flat bristle brush and base coat the piece completely. I find a turntable is helpful to lessen the handling of the piece.

After brushing the base coat into the piece, the brush should be dried as much as possible. I use a paper towel to clean the brush until it leaves only a smudge of color.

Use the dry brush to work in any excess oil on the piece. Keep drying the brush and use it to work in the base coat.

A front view of the stained piece before coloring.

A back view of the stained piece before color is added.

Immediately after base coating, begin with your color coats. Paint the face first. My mixture is made from dabs of burnt sienna, rose madder, and flesh. Dip one corner of the brush in burnt sienna and the other corner in rose madder then mix the two in with the flesh. Add a little linseed oil to thin slightly. More oil will give a thinner, lighter color.

The three colors blended on the plate.

49

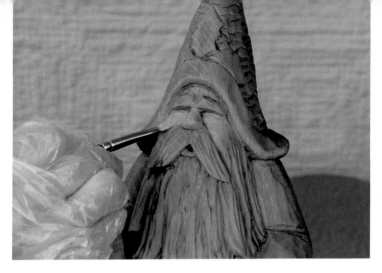

Apply the flesh mixture to the skin areas of the face with a #3 brush and to the lip with a #2/0 detail brush.

Use the same flesh mixture to paint the hands as was used on the face.

Blend a small amount of the rose madder into the flesh on the cheeks and also into the corners of the lower lip to shade and give them more color.

Mix titanium white and linseed oil so that the white is a runny consistency. Paint the beard and eyebrows with the mixture. Use a dry brush to work the white into the base coat to get a two-tone effect.

Base coat the hands while the base coat mixture is still out.

Use this white on any other areas that you intend to be white. Here the heart on Gustave's front is white.

The heart on his back will be painted white as well.

Use thalo green with a #3 flat brush to darken or shade the edges.

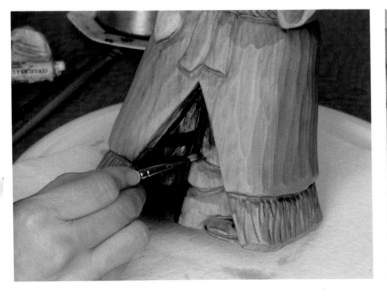

Blend sap green and thalo green with a palette knife in equal amounts and thin with linseed oil. Paint the pant legs.

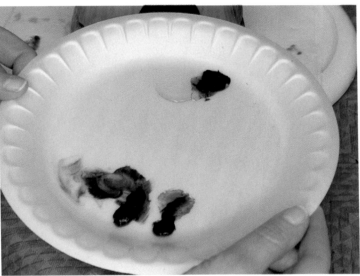

Alazar Crimson red straight from the tube is thinned with linseed oil. Here it is shown on the same mixing plate with the green. Do not allow the green and crimson to mix. The red appears more brown in these photos but it is a dark red.

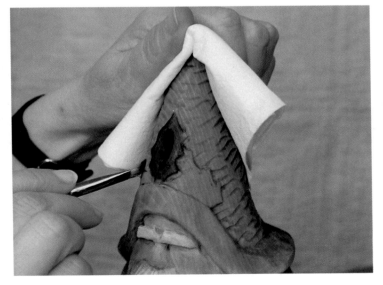

Paint holly leaves with the same green as pants. Remove excess paint from pant legs and holly leaves with a paper towel or Q-Tip.

Apply Alazar Crimson with a #10 brush to the coat area of Gustave.

Paint the open areas first. Use the #3 brush to "cut-in" boundary areas and tight spots.

Put a dab of burnt sienna on a plate and a squirt of linseed oil. Don't mix them.

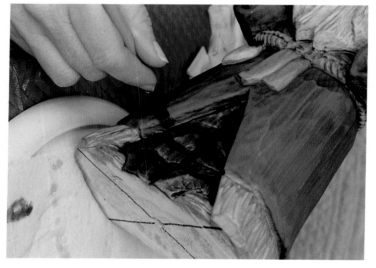

Coat the brush with linseed oil then touch it to a paper towel to absorb the excess. Pick up a dab of burnt sienna and work into the brush by pressing back and forth on a paper towel. There should now be a light load of paint on the brush. Shade as shown around the top of the fur.

Tip the piece to reach tight spots and "cut-in" with the #3 brush.

Cushion the head with paper towels. Tip the piece and find all un-painted areas.

Shade the hanging rope ends.

Shade the top, bottom, and between the coils of the rope belt.

Shade around the ivy and heart.

Shade the inner hood.

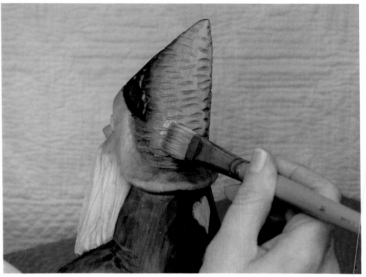

Shade around the hood edges. Feather the shading out into the open areas of the hood.

Shade the soles of the boots and the shadowed areas of the boots.

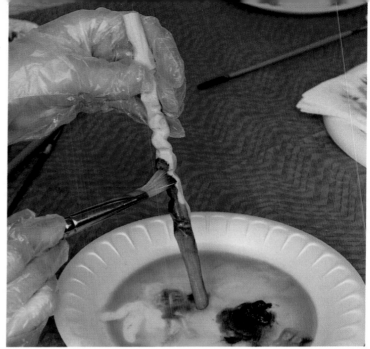

Use paper towels to rub excess paint off the stick.

Using some Payne's grey mixed with linseed oil, shade under the belt, in the arm creases, and around the edge of coat. This helps with the illusion of shadows.

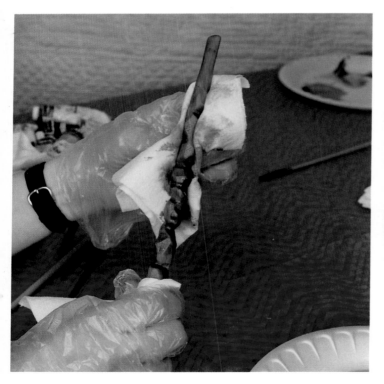

Paint the walking stick with the burnt sienna also.

Move the piece to a well ventilated warm area (preferably outdoors if it is warm enough). Use Grumbacher Tuffilm final fixative matte finish and spray the piece. Let it dry approximately 15 minutes between coats. Rub the piece with a soft cloth between coats. Please read the instructions on the can and follow them carefully. We do not spray when the temperature is below 60 degrees since the spray can crystallize. Oil paint can take a long time to dry if left alone. The spray has a drying agent in it that dries the paint in minutes.

For the eyes, it is recommended that you use acrylic craft paints because the oil paint tends to bleed together and does not dry quickly. Always spray oil painted piece before applying acrylic paint since the two are incompatible. The eyes for this carving are the simplest possible. No eyeball has been carved here, this allows the painter complete freedom in placing and finishing the eyes. Note: Please ignore the chip on Gustave's nose. We found it after the photos were taken. It was easily removed.

Using the 2/0 brush, apply a thin line of white acrylic paint.

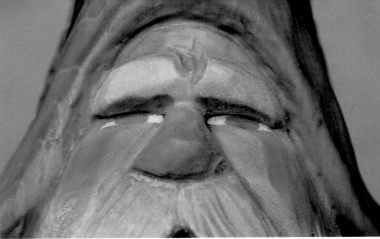

Use medium blue as shown to create the iris area.

Paint in a black pupil as shown.

Put a small white slash on either side of pupil to indicate a light reflection on the eye. Line the top and bottom of the eye with a very thin line of brown madder. Spray the eyes 2 or 3 times and let them dry. Spray the hands and stick also. Glue the hands into the arms and place the stick in the right hand. We do not "antique" these heirloom Santas. You may do so if you wish.

We decorate the finished piece with wreaths, baskets, etc. You can have fun looking in stores for items that are the right scale to add to your figure. Some collectors have even made items for their heirloom Santas. The items shown here were purchased at a craft store.

Back view of Gustave.

Right side view of Gustave.

The Gallery

The figures pictured here are various Santas I have done over the years. Some are over 5 years old and a close inspection will let you see how my work has changed with time.

There are many cast reproduction Santas not pictured in the gallery that are available as study pieces. There are also some precarved wood blanks for the Gustave the Stout project. If you are interested in a cast study piece or in a precarved wood blank, please send $2 for a catalog to Paul F. Bolinger, 4405 S. Echo Ct., Spokane, Wa. 99223.

An 18" Santa in blue. Note the lighter staining and the block treatment at the bottom. Also, this Santa has no walking stick.

A French Santa. Note the more complex eye treatment.

Gustave with two similar-sized Santas.

A 12" Santa. Note that he has no separate hands. Mittens are carved on the figure instead.

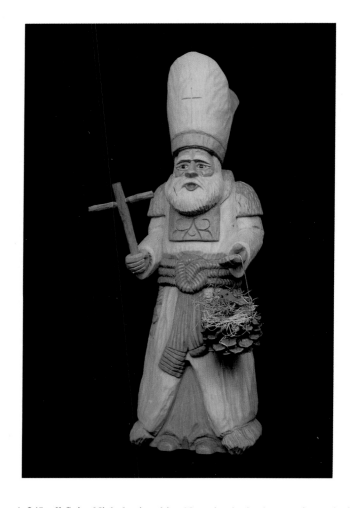

A 24" tall Saint Nicholas in white. Note that he has a cross instead of a walking stick.

Gustave with some larger friends.

Side view of the Santa with the angel walking stick.

A 24" tall Santa with an angel walking stick.

Back view.

St. Francis. Not actually a Santa.

Back view of St. Francis.

Back view of the bishop.

A 14" tall bishop with "crozier" style walking stick.

Santa with a full robe to the ground. Note that no pants or boots show.

An Interesting Story

Part of my work involves traveling the country, making personal appearances in shops to meet customers and collectors. Many of the questions I am asked concern how I became a professional woodcarver. I think the story is interesting enough to be repeated here.

In 1980 a simple Christmas gift changed my life. I was attending a Christmas party given by an associate of my future wife. This woman had a small work area in her home where she was practicing sign carving in order to be able to make some signs for her own use. I was fascinated by the tools and the obvious attraction of the carving process. I guess my fascination showed because that very Christmas another friend, who had been at the same party, gave me a chisel and a block of wood. I began to carve that very day and was immediately hooked. Hardly a day has passed since without me doing some carving. On the days when I can't carve for some reason, I daydream about carving.

It took me about three years of working at my carving skills before I had anything that I was willing to try to sell. My earliest carvings were all simple relief carvings and they were very primitive. I carved them as fast as I could and sold them at the occasional art and wine festival or craft show. I really only sold them in order to get feedback from customers and to get rid of the growing clutter in our small town house. I certainly wasn't doing it for money.

I carved my first Father Christmas at the request of my wife. She had been asking me for some time to make Santas for the stone fireplace mantle at our cottage. I made three Santas and she painted them. We displayed them proudly on the mantle for all to see. I still have these three Santas and they are very primitive. They are also very special to us.

Our neighbor owned a small shop nearby and admired these Santas so much that he was certain he could sell them. I made three more Santas for him to take to his shop and within a day or so he was back to report that all three were sold and he needed more. Ever since that day I have been behind schedule and never will catch up. I really didn't do anything other than Father Christmas figures for years after that.

For several years I carved and sold my Santas as a hobby. As my skills grew, my wife's painting skills grew too. Eventually she began experimenting with oil painting on the wooden Santas. After several years she had perfected a technique for oil painting that provided a deep lustrous finish for our pieces that made them stand apart from others. Prices for our Santas increased and demand kept going up. In addition to being popular with our customers, our Father Christmas figures gained notice with national magazine editors and we soon found ourselves the subjects of articles and features in many magazines.

At some point along the way we realized that it might be possible for me to become a professional woodcarver. We planned for that day by working on outlets for our work and establishing a relationship with Kurt S. Adler, Inc. of New York to reproduce and distribute reproductions for us. The great, and scary, day came in 1992 when I decided to give up my job as vice president of a San Jose, California computer chip manufacturer and begin my life as a professional woodcarver.

Today we find ourselves designing Santas and other figures that are reproduced and sold in the U.S. and Canada. We have thousands of collectors and each year many more people find our work and begin to collect. All of that came from the simple gift of a friend.

Here are some of our accomplishments:

- twice selected among America's best traditional craftsmen by *Early American Life* magazine;
- twice selected as creating the year's best Christmas figure by *Early American Life* magazine;
- featured in the book <u>An Old Fashioned Christmas</u> by the staff of *Country Home* magazine;
- published the children's Christmas book <u>The Forever Wreath</u> which was selected as the Christmas bedtime story by *Country Living* magazine;
- and featured in various magazines including Better Homes & Gardens *Christmas Ideas* magazine, Better Homes & Gardens *Santa Claus* magazine, *Collector's Editions* magazine, *Collector's Mart* magazine, and others.